SHOUT MAMMY SHOUT

WHERE THE THUNDER HIDES

TrubuPRESS is a subsidiary of the Trubu Media Group whose interests include but are not limited to fiction and non fiction stories from the black experience throughout the American and African Diaspora.

Publisher: TrubuPRESS
Editor: Neo Blaqness
Cover Design: TrubuPRESS
Proofreader: Tamika Coleman

SHOUT MAMMY SHOUT: Where The Thunder Hides
Second Edition
Copyright © 2014 Yolantha Harrison-Pace

To order SHOUT MAMMY SHOUT: Where The Thunder Hides visit http: //trubupress.com
or call (872) 22TRUBU

Booksellers:
Retail discounts are available from TrubuPRESS. Inquiries about volume orders can be made via the phone number listed above.

ISBN-13: 978-0615974934
ISBN-10: 0615974937
Published by TrubuPRESS

PRINTED IN THE UNITED STATES

This book is dedicated to my daddy,

Raphael A. Harrison, Sr.

His father, Granddaddy Joe,
and to my grandfather on my mother's side,
Professor E. H. Henry

CONTENTS

CONTENTS

CONTENTS

CONTENTS

CONTENTS

INTRODUCTION

I am a product of violence. I grew up with corporal punishment- that's when beating hitting, kicking, slapping, screaming at, cussing, shoving, head thumping—just to name a few were consequences for "bad behavior" and used as legal methods by parents for parental control) Therefore when my husband was abusive the same exhibition of strategies for power and control over me just seemed like natural consequences.

Another strategy of control is to destroy a person's ability to think and speak for themselves. This strategy squelches the persons ability to express an "original thought." I became a survivor of my childhood abuse when I left home and went to college.

I became a survivor of my spousal abuse when I left my house under police escort after coming home to a chainsaw and a hole cut where my refrigerator once stood in which I surmised was cut to deposit the remains of my body.

Once I left these abusive situations I took on the mantel of SURVIVOR. I even spoke to and counseled other ABUSED women and children, encouraging and inspiring them to become SURVIVORS. I excelled at talking SURVIVOR TALK. Somehow, deep in my ovaries, deep in the gut of my female humanity being a SURVIVOR was not enough.

I always felt as if I was dressed inappropriately but no one had shared the dress code. I felt like I was eating with plastic utensils while everyone else was using the good china. It was as if the playing field was tilted or as if the rules of the game changed daily and I didn't get the memo. I had become a SURVIVOR EXTRAORDINAIRE, but where was the VICTORY? Where was the fine china of my life?

I began to partake of the exquisite meals and don the designer suits of my life when I dared to take back my voice. I began to shine when I started to think my own thoughts, ferret out my own conclusions. The ultimate change came when I began to speak out in victory venues, at "grown-up" tables and not just at sad sack pity party events. I needed documentation, a strategy, proof of the precious victory pudding. And as trite as it might sound, I had to learn to crawl before I could walk, then skip then run.

The crawl of my voice began as a soft purr, then a whisper, then monologues of self talk, then shared dialogues. This book is my documentation of my voice. It is a celebration of "not an ABUSED me, not a SURVIVOR me, but of me recovering and celebrating my voice of VICTORY. This book is a necessary sequel to my very first book as the quintessential survivor, WING-PLUCKED BUTTERFLY: one woman's war on hate crimes against women and children. This book is my victorious thunder. When I unchained myself and boldly let myself out...I began to dance and swish the hem of my dress and I began to SHOUT, MAMMY, SHOUT!!!

As a child, thunder always intrigued me. It's magic sound embraced unanswerable questions. Just one BA-BOOOOOOM could scare the bejeezus out of the strongest and stoutest of people I knew...stop them in their tracks. I've seen thunder turn a grown man into a crying-blathering-superstitious-pulling-the-cover-over-his-head-getting-off-the-phone-cause-its-starting-to-thunder-200-pound-weakling. I never understood that because to me thunder was beautiful… bodacious and unabashedly beautiful. I remember dreaming as a little colored girl in Amarillo, Texas, "one day when I grow up I want to be just like thunder."

As I became older I felt my thunder---meaning caused so much fear that people actually stopped in their tracks. I became thunderous when I asked questions or challenged the status quo or when I chose to not stand wrong with the crowd, but chose to stand for right…all alone. In my meager fifty years, I've asked questions that adjourned meetings within 15 minutes of having been convened.

I've asked questions challenging the status quo that cleared off whole pews at church, questions that caused a 10-minute recess at a trial (aren't I suppose to have a lawyer present?) I've asked questions regarding right and wrong that shut down dormitory cafeterias, questions that made me friendless (they were probably only long time acquaintances any how). Questions in which I really meant no harm, I was just wondering or trying to engage in a win-win conversation that would produce a win-win solution. Never the less folks responded as if they had been hit with a clap of thunder.

In my thunderous naiveté I don't see anything wrong with asking:

Have you ever suffered the blues from A-Z?

Did September 11 make you forget your Christianity?

Are you sleeping with the enemy?

What are you gonna do about all of our 'brothas' in prison?

Whaz up with cross gendering?

What if you had the faith of an avocado seed?

Is God's covenant alive and well today?

Who says God is a man?

Is denial really all that bad?

What happened to sister love?

Have you ever considered suicide?

Didn't there use to be more rainbows?

Why has the world gone crazy?

Have we forgotten the power of the Black Woman?

The following pages approach a few of these questions and more. Welcome to my book of thunder, I would one-day love to read yours.

Let The Thunder Roll!!!

ACKNOWLEDGEMENTS

*M*en like my daddy are exceptional. Men like my daddy are an endangered species and in some communities, men like my daddy are out and out extinct. My father did not send us to church, he took us. He taught Sunday School and he even joined us on the pew for Sunday morning worship services. I learned that the most valuable thing a man can do is to attend church with his loved ones.

Daddy's consistent presence at home and at church taught me about the omnipresence of God. I believe children, Black or White, Hispanic or Viet-Namese, Haitian or otherwise, who are raised in this kind of environment grow up to be exceptional children. My four brothers and I, Raphael, Jr., Thaxter, Xerxes and Burdick are not perfect children by any means, but we are exceptional children indeed.

Another awesome phenomenon in my life is that I knew both of my grandfathers. They too were devout, church-going, Christian men. Granddaddy Joe, passed away in his easy chair studying his Sunday School lesson. Daddy also grew up around his father's father. Great Grandfather David was instrumental in building my father's strong spiritual foundation through the Bible.

But of my grandfathers, I knew my mother's dad the best. For I grew up seeing my grandfather, Professor E. H. Henry, pray, lead devotionals and pass the offering plate in an "ol'

ACKNOWLEDGEMENTS

timey religion" country church. A church where the women sat on one side and the men sat on the other, way out in the bottom in Elm Grove, Texas.

These gloriously exceptional men sparked the lightening that gave me the boldness to recognize God's lightening filled love in my life. May this book be…my thunderous thank you.

SHOUT MAMMY SHOUT

WHERE THE THUNDER HIDES

Yolantha Harrison Pace

TRUBU PRESS
A Black Legacy Publishing Company

Psalm 81:7...

*"you cried to me in trouble and I saved you.
I answered from Mount Sinai
where the thunder hides."*

Where The Thunder Hides

A tisket, a tasket
A lightening filled basket
Thunder, are you here?
Within each person
Abides the roar of thunder
Waiting to be unleashed
Oooooooohh thuuuuuuuundeeeer
Come out, come out
Wherever you are.
Tragedy abounds
When thunderous power
Lies dormant, sedated
From the bowels of a grave
A nightmare posing in the daylight
Thunder are you there?
Ah--you scared !!!

God's grace of forgiveness
Is the resurrected Holy Ghost
Banished to live…
Where the thunder hides.

Professor E. H. Henry

My mother's father, born in 1895, was a phenomenal man. Having to support his family at an early age, he did not graduate high school until he was 21 years old. He met my grandmother at Prairie View A & M College. Grandmother was an exquisite woman with a melodious voice who loved to read. And the most beautiful picture in the universe was to watch and listen to her read to Grandfather, and oh how he loved to hear her read.

Everybody had a Professor E. H. Henry story. He was the first and only "colored" principal of his day. Every body respected him, revered him and many, especially his students, even feared him. White people, sheriffs, administrators, and politicians wooed him as "the" Negro leader. Grandfather was the barometer for the African American community. Politicians knew that if they had E. H. Henry on their side, they had the entire "colored" vote. However, Grandfather was a man of the utmost integrity, he might be on your side but he never rode in anyone's pocket.

My last memory of Grandfather was when he came to Austin to see me graduate with my Bachelors of Fine Arts with Honors degree. He walked around the University of Texas with his hands behind his back as if he was the campus President. When Grandfather died at the age of 89 it was the end of an American Era. There was no one left to carry on with his uncompromising passion and compassion for his people. There was no one of his thunderous caliber to step into his well-worn shoes.

"Prof"

Grandfather lived by ritual
Not habit, but ritual
Habit is doing, just for the doing
Ritual is doing for a specified purpose
Grandfather called Grandmother, Kid
And Grandmother did the same to Grandfather
I never ever saw Grandfather smile
I remember him making others laugh with delight
But he, himself,
never showed pleasure in his own ingenuity
Every meal when there were children at the table
And even sometimes when it was just he and Kid
He would ask without ever
Breaking his eating stride
"Is it good?"
Then after a hearty yes from his audience
He'd let out a deep soft guttural
King of the jungle roar
"Eeeeeeeee-eat it."
We would all squeal with delight
He would sop, without changing his game face,
His bread in the homemade syrup
Mixed with sausage grease from a pig

he himself had raised and slaughtered
We had the honor of calling him Grandfather
His closest friends called him "Prof"
But never to his face
He was always addressed as
Professor Henry
He epitomized education
Specifically the education of colored children
In Texas he was a power-wielding charter member
of The NAACP National Association for
the Advancement of Colored People
And a mighty member of the Urban League
Human rights were his passion
At a time when these organizations
Reorganized America
Unlike today when these organizations meet
In order to organize meetings
Grandfather got up every morning before anybody
Walked his property
Ate breakfast
Milked the cows
Then spent his day
Doing his farming ritual
Which sometimes included
Riding like a king on top
Of his yellow John Deere throne
Grandfather,
Professor E. H. Henry,
Was a
MAN OF THUNDER.

Snaaaaaaaaaaake

City slickers, city slickers,
And then humiliating laughter
All daylong
Chanted and laughed my
Country cousins
Everything my four brothers and I said
Was city dumb
And provoked country laughter
Grandfather walked by
"You kids need to be out there picking cotton"
My country cousins scattered
My brothers took their cue from my cousins
I was left standing in their dust
Squinting from the country sun
Watching Grandfather with his dignified country walk
Go into the barn
I imitated his walk, as best I could
Following him into the barn
He climbed up into the loft
Grandfather knew I was there
Without even letting me know
That he knew I was there
Thus began my country education.

I climbed to the first level
He went up another level and
Tossed down a bale of hay
"Hay," Grandfather said
The smell of it itched my nose
so badly I sneezed
"Snake" said Grandfather
Without breaking the stride
of his every day voice
And he threw it down
It floated down in slow motion
like in a nightmare
I screamed and hopped
and jumped and jerked
Like a city slicker
Snaaaaaaake, snaaaaaaake, snaaaaaaake
I didn't care;
I'd never seen a country snake
Let alone ever had any kind of snake
Country, city, continental,
island or other wise
Float down to my feet
When I was semi calm
Grandfather picked up the airy snake
And educated me on
How a snake sheds its skin
My grandfather
was full of thunderous knowledge

Pickin Cotton

I was probably,
Nine, ten, or eleven
But I know
It was before I was thirteen
I got up city early
Turns out I was country late
Everyone else was way down their rows
I went down to catch up with the others
Grandfather sent me back
"Start at the beginning
Never start at the middle
Never start at the middle of the beginning
Or the beginning of the end
Always start
At the beginning of the beginning
You have two rows
One on each side of you
You pick the left behind cotton."
Eeeeeee-yew worms
Worms were everywhere
Little tiny silky green ones
Brown speckled knobby-kneed ones
Closing my eyes

I wasn't gonna act like a city slicker
This city country gal
Was gonna pick some cotton
My country cousins on their
Country rusty bicycles pumping
Three to a bike
Rode by with country laughter
And squealed at me with
Country menace
"Watch out for snaa-akes"
"I ain't scared no snakes," I whispered back
"And spiiii-duhs" they tossed over their shoulders
And sped off.
Oh no.
No sooner had they said that
That I began to see "spiiii-duhs"
Everywhere
Then I saw a spider on the ground eating a worm
I jumped over it, yes indeed,
spiders were my friends
I scooted around another one
And commenced to
Picking cotton
It was a hard task
The cotton holders were sharp
Bolls they were called
And you had to pull the cotton
Out just right
Or it snagged and left some
Behind in the sharpness of
The bolls

Grandfather, inspected my work
He made me go back to the beginning
Of the beginning twice
Because of my leaving behind
Some of the 'left behind'
The burlap sack mixed with city sweat
Itched my neck
And made whelps on my skin
And gave a prickly feel to the inside
Smelling part of my nose
The tears started inching out
Of my eye corners
Picking cotton hurt
I was wearing one of
Grandfather's long sleeve tan shirts
I wiped my face on the sleeve
My city nose took notice of the smell
I smelled like grandfather
That gave me the strength to pick on
The other pickers were way down at a distance
And looked like a postcard I once saw
That read
"Coloreds Picking Cotton"
For the first time in my life
I now understood what colored meant
Day was up
And it was weighing time
Grandfather latched the burlap bags
On a hook scale on the back of his truck
Called out a name and a price
Then paid the people

Nicholas Shorter--ten dollars
Rudolph Henry--17 dollars
Melvina Hurd--23 dollars and seventy-five cents
The other pickers went, "Humph"
I sat waiting my turn
And almost fell asleep
On my bag
I was so tired I didn't
Feel its scratchiness any more
"Little Henry-Harrison"
I barely could stand up
He took my sack
Dragged it over to the hook
Lifted it up with all of his might
He glared out at the crowd with pride
"My Granddaughter,
Little Henry-Harrison--fifty cents"
I felt the laughter in the air
But no body dared
I climbed onto the truck bed
Grandfather gave me two shiny quarters
Without taking his thunderous eyes
Off of the other cotton pickers
I loved my grandfather
And I never told him.

Mountains of a
Black Mole Hill Woman

I was born, raised and married into physical, emotional and economic abuse. It was the grace of the Kentucky Mountains that healed the wounds of my bleeding soul. These mountains reminded me that I was forgiven.

These mountains reminded me to forgive myself and they reminded me to be forgiving. These majestic mountains, from the knobs west of Danville to the blessed back trails of Beattyville, to the voluptuous valleys of Virgie, gave me reason to wake up, get out of bed and to go on living another day.

God's Prerogative

The Kentucky Angel asked
"Why make a mountain?
Wasn't the valley enough?
You've got oceans of stuff,
Rivers of fish,
What else could you wish?"
The Blue Grass Angel chided God,
"You have enough to do
With forests and firmament
And nature's brew."
God smiled real plain
And giggled hee-hee, ha-hew
"I'm making mountains
just cause…
I want to."

Sleeping Mountainsourus

Her grassy body covered
In multi-tones of green
Adorned with Hippy wildflowers
Her rock teeth
Have gnawed her
Niche along the valley plain
A tree-do of bangs tossed back
In a Farrah Faucett shag
Trimmed every three-months
In natures salon
She sleeps
Dreaming of her ancestors of
Volcanoes past

They Call Me Appalachia

Trampled
Scrutinized with the
Naked eye of longing
My sacred secrets exposed
My veins ripped
Torn and stripped
Of my precious black gold
Violated…
Yet I survive with my dignity intact
Supporting and sustaining life
Providing for the earth
In spite of my raped bowels
In spite of the highways
That tear through my thighs
And the pitiful finger machines
That claw at my mountain dress
Man passes on but
I am the ultimate mountain woman
Still rising to the sky
I remain
My leaf tips blood stained
Yet and still
Appalachia is my name.

Mountain Everlasting

Mountain high
Mountain low
Round the bend
The Angels know
Secrets of Joy
Secrets of Pain
A People strong
A People slain
Keeping histories
Of days gone past
Though People perish
Mountain Memories last

God's Mistress

God's mistress
Is a mountain
A mistress
Above all mistresses
Loyal beautiful
Giving reckless
Love without
Abandon with
Natural things
Her flirtatious streams
Her whistling robins
Her dewdrop tree lashes
Her misty jeweled fog
Her spectrum of greenery
And rainbow autumn breath
For God knows
When a mountain hugs you
You remain forever caressed.

...the Kentucky Angel
Asked God once more and again,
"...and why make a mountain..."?
God smiled back patiently
"Because...I can, because I can!"

Kentucky Goddess

Nothing on earth
Tops her splendor
No place else
Can God render
White butterfly dust
From angels wings
That rolls up
And changes things
Then lifts without schedule
A new day to unveil
The beauty of heaven
That overrides hell
An early mountain ride
Between dusk and dawn
Yields angels lounging in trees
Their footsteps on the greenacious lawn
The third side of time
Where autumn tends to fall
She shows us glimpses
In God's color call
The richness of rainbow
Spattered on the leaves
What other mighty magic

Is up her celestial sleeve
Playing hide and seek
With God's sunshine treasure
Unfolding beauty
Without measure
Echoing her lovers love
Who lives on high
A Black Mountain goddess
Dropped from above
To kiss the Kentucky sky.

Death Valley

*I*n my high school year of 1972-1973, I participated in my coming out party--a cotillion ball for young African American girls. My name and parent's names appeared in the local paper. Not soon after the news article, I received a letter from prison. In my naiveté, I wrote back and gained a pen pal. Or so I thought.

After about 6 months of correspondence, he was being released and wanted to meet me and run off together. He had "plenty of money saved up from a robbery he had committed." I freaked out as only a nice, sheltered 16-year-old Christian girl would do. I wrote him that I was going off to college and I didn't think it would work out. I stopped writing. I didn't hear from him again.

Two years later I became Miss Columbia College of Columbia, Missouri. My name and parent's names appeared once again in the Champaign-Urbana local paper. Like before, I received a letter from a prison inmate. I knew better than to write back.

About six years ago, I had one of my first articles published in "Bamboo Girls", a feminist magazine.

And you guessed it I received a letter from a gentleman in prison, this time on death row. Being in my 40's, I thought I was mature enough to handle the pen pal friendship. But I wasn't, so I ended the demanding correspondences. Somewhere I saved the letters, hidden only to be found after I'm dead and gone. But through my journals, I have kept within reach some of my responses to this thunderous relationship. Here's to Death Row Reggie...

Death Valley Sonata

Another Brotha Bites The Dust In Five Movements

MOVEMENT #I

Mama's Allegro

I still set a plate for you
3 times a day, everyday
And at night
Pop enough popcorn
For you to enjoy overflowing handfuls
Reggie…time to get up
Do you smell the thick slabs of bacon?
Dancing in their juices
Do you smell the Texas toast?
Broiling perfect cubes of butter
Making a patchwork quilt of delight?
To ooze a shiny stream down the back of your
Cast iron ebony knuckles
With the first warm bite?
Yes! That's sausage, too
Twanged with chili pepper and sage and a dollop of vinegar
To salsa between your teeth and make
Firecrackers of your tongue
Reggie--Breakfast!
Maybe, I'll see you for lunch

For a thick fried bologna, egg, and cheese sandwich
Although it ain't quite the same
Since the gov'mint went out of the cheese business
But, I'll doctor it up with 3 valentine red slices of tomato
Straight out of my garden
Just for you.
I'll sugar coat and pepper the rest to watch you slurp down
Juices caught at the last second with a gulp
I liked feeding you,
'Cause you never wasted mama's food
on store bought napkins or
Stiff sinful paper towels
Lunchtime, Reggie…Reggie?
And dinner
I'm frying again
With the grease from this morning's bacon
A whole chicken cut into half
And 2 halves again.
With gravy from the drippings
Dimpled with barely visible
Melt in your mouth fantasy lumps of taste
I'm ovening up some potatoes,
With corn pudding to lean up against
my garden black eye peas with
Flecks of string beans and butterbeans tangoing in the pot.
Do you smell mama's thick cake corn bread?
It's time to wash your hands.
Reggie…dinner's serve.
Reh--gee? Come on down and eat boy
Yo' foods gittin' cold.
Reginald P. Thomas Saint John the Baptist the Third!!!

Don't you hear me calling you boy?

…and every Christmas

I put out a carrot for Rudolph

And homemade raisin 'n' oatmeal cookies

And a tall glass of milk for Santa!!!

Reggie, sleep tight, don't let the prison bugs bite

Good night, son, good night.

MOVEMENT #2

Death Valley Adagio

(Death Row Angel)

Her vapor whispers down

The stream

Corn rowed with woolen flaxed hair

Banister like baldness

Cotton rowed with defeat

Rows of dumbbells and

Brawny shells

Pretty little man maidens

All in a row

Shelved

Finely chiseled museum pieces

Of debonair, crème de la crème

Mocha black men

Blockbustered at death's video store

She pauses in front of this one

Hell argues with heaven

At the nape of his neck

Hummingbirds flutter in his hair

The tickling of a hazel nut colored sugar ant
Stings his soul
Properly measured
Lethal legality pitches him into a confused high
He downward tumbles into unspoken depths
Grotesque mouths sing silently
Somewhere a mother shouts herself into oblivion
Another brown woman's son just checked out
Of the library congress of death.

MOVEMENT #3

Bed Time Stories

(Chewin' Duh Fat & Death Valley Chat)

His tongue is heavy
Like a full set of encyclopedias
All thick like the Bible
And shaped like the Koran
Rapped in the poetical religion
Of the penal code
Yet he raps like there's no tomorrow
Shuckin' and jivin'
Knowing tomorrow's yesterdays
Will never come
But like the long lost
and forgotten griot
He reinvents reality
to the viable present
From tattered magazines
Caked with the crimes

Of other men's hands
All ears turn toward the poet
In his cell down the way
As they hold their
Manhood's tightly
"To laugh with her
Is an audible expression of proof
That I still listen to her
No matter how you shape it
Funny is divine intimacy
An outward expression
Of the joy at being
In one another's presence
She always knows it's over
When we stop laughing
I know it is over when I smile
At another man's woman"
The death row men relieve themselves
In unison
At the thought of the days
When they too juggled
two women at a time
They'll all sleep good tonight

MOVEMENT #4

Death Valley Minuet

(Mama Got Shot)

She didn't say goodbye
'cause you weren't there
Not because she didn't want to
Tell you..
Or embrace you…
But because you weren't there
While some other thug shot up
Your neighborhood
What gun were you shootin' last night
While your mama lay dying
Bathing in the blood that once
Rocked you?
There was a killing
in the hood
And nobody cared,
Nobody dared
Some black man in a hurry
To see Reggie
He got his Reggie on
Taking down a whole row
of Reggie seeds with him
The Reggians worship
the Reggie god of their existence
Their Reggie pharaoh
When will the Reggie Moses come
and let my brothas go?

MOVEMENT #5

Death Valley Scherzo
(Reggie's Execution)

On that none day in history
In every kitchen that had fed Reggie
For a moment
Bacon refused to fry
Yeast refused to rise
Butter acted like margarine
Gallon jugs of milk
Spilled themselves in the refrigerator.
In every bathroom that had bathed Reggie
Lipsticks refused to come out of their designer tubes
Toothbrushes curled up into petrified plastic balls
Toilets flushed themselves repeatedly
Bathtubs filled themselves and overflowed.
In all of the bedrooms that had slept his body
Dresser drawers sprang open in unison
Unmatched socks curled up to their mates
And mattresses gave off the stench of rain.
While all of Reggie's women met
with their teeth unbrushed
And their lips unstained
Round the drinking fountain
To laugh at their remembrances of
"…that time when Reggie…"

September 11th

September 11, 2001

I couldn't understand why September 11, 2001 put me a black woman who lived 4 states away in a fetal position, emotionally petrified and drowning in the putrefying smell of hopelessness.

It cast me into a spiraling depression I had not felt sense February 11, 1988 when I left my abusive husband. As I watched the towers crumble time and time again and felt myself caving in upon the rawness of my soul, it took another fellow warrior and survivor of domestic violence to snatch me back into a healing reality.

Her calming spirit reminded me that I had spent 10 years ensnared by my terrorist. Ten years in which I was sleeping with the enemy. The loudest kept secret in America is our at home, daily, residential, domestic war of terrorism that goes on methodically in our communities.

Our silence endorses the secret guerilla warfare that goes on behind closed doors, the accepted hush-hush hate crimes perpetuated against women every 9 seconds of our red, white and blue minute. My fight back from the insanity of September 11 came through the healing medicine of journaling. Because that horrendous day in America left me…

Sleepless In Kentucky

For that which I am about to say,
I am most afraid.
In 46 years
I have never known me this way…
Sleepless, tasteless, zombied out.
I have lived through
some phenomenal experiences,
However;
September 11
Changed my life
It changed my perspective of me drastically.
This is a quest
to introduce myself to the new me.
For that which I am about to say,
I am most afraid.
Because for a moment
I descended into insomniac madness.
I AM SLEEPLESS IN KENTUCKY

Day 1
TUESDAY, SEPTEMBER 11, 2001

Am I Dead

Oh no, oh no,
What am I seeing?
Who did that?
WHO DID THAT?
There was this building
I had the chance to visit as a tourist
But I had to choose between the
Statue of liberty and the twin trade towers
I chose lady liberty
I had always wondered if I'd made the right choice
My heart is doing belly flops and
It isn't even part of my digestive system
It is as if my intestines are swallowing for me
My eyes are stretched to behind my ears
And my feet are deaf
I am hearing upside down
I smell inside out
I am breathing through my fingertips
Who is this person?
AM I DEAD?
Am I one of the 5000 unaccounted for?
Crushed and burned and churned
Have I risen with the ashes?

I've been smoked
Blown into action
By the terminator
Becoming my own
Action hero
To protect the children
In my immediate
Concentric circle of concern
I am chest expanded in slow motion
HEEEEEEEEELP ME!
I am numb

Little Liza

ome here little Liza
Remember how you always wanted to
come over to Miz. Pace house?
Well today is your day.

Did mommy finally say yes?

Well, yes she did.

Oh Mix Pace, can I stay the night?

Well would you like to spend two nights?

Oh could I, could I? Will Mamma let me?

Well…yes…she will.

Oh gee, oh gee. Let's go, let's go.

Well, yes, let's go.

Maybe we could play a joke on mommy and I could stay with you a long time, without telling mom.

Why would you want to do that?

Well Momma works so hard all day, and when she comes home at night she is so very tired. She doesn't have time for me, so usually I fall asleep in the car on the way home after I eat what momma brought me from her job at the twin tower restaurant. You are a lot of fun, you are not like all of my other babysitters, would you like to keeeeep me? I could be yours.

Well, maybe for a little while. We'll have to pray about

that.

I don't think mommy would mind she needs a break. And we'll have lots of fun. Maybe if I stay with you, tomorrow night, mommy can go back to the Windows of the World restaurant as a customer instead of as a waitress, she is always saying that one day she is going to go do that, put on her best dress and walk into the world trade center, go right up to the 107th floor where she works, sit down and let someone wait on her for a change.

Liza???…

Yes Mix Pace???…Are you crying?

…get your backpack

You are crying, well that's good, that will give me something special to do tonight, I'm good at making my mamma feel good, and making her laugh and making her forget? Have you got something you want to forget? I'm good at doing that.

Little Liza…well, maybe you should stay with me until I can forget.

Day 2
WEDNESDAY, SEPTEMBER 12, 2001

Up All Night

Did I stay up all night?
I don't remember
I cannot dance
I cannot sing
I cannot walk
I cannot hum
I cannot cry
Should I have peas?
Should I have carrots?
Should I run to the piggly wiggly
and get peas and carrots mixed?
I'm staring into the refrigerator
What did I want?
Maybe I was going into the freezer
I look there
It is smoky
Like the news reports on television
I slam the freezer door
It's 2:37 a.m.
7:45 a.m. At work
I give empty hugs
I stare into over bugged out eyes of
Wondering school children

Looking to me
For comfort
I will not frown
I will not flinch
3:32 p.m.
A brave psychotic new look
I see mirrored in
Women all around me
My face, my mind, my heart
Have redesigned themselves

Day 3
THURSDAY, SEPTEMBER 13, 2001

Moaning

I only moan
I am shoulder rounded
I rock to and fro
Back and forth
In the rocking chair of my soul
I only moan
I am shoulder rounded
I rock to and fro
Back and forth
In the rocking chair of my soul
I only moan
I am shoulder rounded
I rock to and fro
Back and forth
In the rocking chair of my soul
I am a womb tomb
I only moan

Diminishing Returns

Not to diminish
Any man's anguish
But right now I am
Too pained
To speak from any ones perspective
But my own
I am a woman under siege
As I pass other women
We don't smile
We don't laugh
I haven't head a giggle in the last 3 days
And most women I now meet
Like me, have horizontal lips

Queen Liberty

How do you get up
Queen liberty
Relight your torch
Brush off the thick clay dust
Tattered and torn
Your heart shattered and worn
Menstruating from every pore
As a sign of your fertility
Your ripeness for a new dawn
Yet you have been shoved to your knees, raped
And your face rubbed in the concrete
of your own foundation
Yet like the black woman you are
You hitch up your bosom
Yet like the Native American you are
Your skirt fans the smoke
Signals of freedom
Your Alamo outcries and
Little Big Horn loyalties
Unite abruptly
Like the immigrant woman you are
You grit your teeth
Wipe your hands on the apron of your

Sacred burial ground agonies
Down rooted and tumbled
You prepare the last meal
A wake
For your twin tower children of spent cries
Deep southern fried chicken
Snuggled up beside German potato salad
Neighboring with little shrimplets
Riding upon a cushion of White House fried rice
Saluted by a slab of Mexican cornbread
You have so much to say
But you own a new sorrow
No words invented can express

Don't Cry

Don't cry lady liberty
You did your best
You just looked away for
A few horrific minutes
Like at a picnic
When everyone thinks
Everyone else is watching
The children
And then little Billy drowns
Because we all looked away
For a few horrific unattended seconds.

Day 4
FRIDAY, SEPTEMBER 14, 2001

The Terrorists are Coming

A patriot call was declared
A day of mourning
Calling all patriots
Calling all patriots
The terrorists are coming
The terrorists are coming
The terrorists are coming
The terrorists are coming

Keys and Candle Light Vigils

What can a candle do
Give me a torch
I'm mad as hell now
My temple has been overturned
By unrighteous bastards
I cannot find my keys
To my prayers
I cannot find my keys
To my anger without sin
I check the back of the front door knobs
I check the kitchen table
I check every closet pocket like
A crazy madwoman
Searching for my wisdom keys
I scratch and tear at the rubble of my
Two twin breast towers
My keys are not there
I sit in the middle of
The cyclone of my terror
Screaming to heaven
Where are my keys
I can't be late
The children are waiting for me

I hear the slight jingle
I was holding my keys
in my left hand all the time

The Power of Hair

When I couldn't make sense of things
I used to cut my hair
Change its color
Do something 'follically' drastic
In order to cope with
My chaotic surroundings
I donned a new look
As if a new person
Who has shed the snakeskin
Of her pain
This time I'm not
Cutting, dying, braiding, hot combing,
Jeri curling, twist locking nothing
I ain't changing a thang
Bring on the ball game

Birthing a Nation
Or My Country Too

(Part 1)

My mammy strong arms

Embraced, encircled and suckled

A step-nation of children

Til' with the grace of time

This became my country, too

I give you again my diligence, dedication,

and tenacious tenacity

I give you again

my African spider like wisdom to pursue

The righteous consequences

of justice, unflinched

With no regrets, looking back

On the red, white, and blue bravery

Bathed with blood

That birthed this, my country tis of me

This is my country, too

Day 5
SATURDAY, SEPTEMBER 15, 2001

Claustrophobia

I gotta get out
I gotta get out
I gottagetoutIgottagetoutIgottagetout

Out The Window from My Toilet Seat

I hear Noah's birds
Singing a butterfly song
In between the drips
Of tears from my leaky upstairs bathtub faucet
Leaves are shedding their green
For a new wardrobe
A squirrel scampers anxiously
In the smell of her new autumn home
Cars pass, as if they are
Going somewhere again
The cartoons are on next door
I feel the red, white, and blue
blood of my blackness
Coagulating into hope
Don't look left
Don't look right
Every thing's gonna be all right
Sound off 1-2
Sound off 3-4
1234
1-2
THREE-FOUR

My Country Too (Part 2)

Enclosed and embodied
By tobacco grass and amber Appalachia
Covered by skies of Nat King Cole blue
Bombtombed by terrorist acts
Emotionally roller coasted
Hey, Mr. President
(tune of Happy Birthday)
This is my country, too
This is my country, too
This is my country, tooooooo
This is my country, too
(blow big fat kiss)
People of brown
Melted into rainbow ashes
Negroes, coloreds, afros, blondes, hair woven, permed
Braided, tinted, conked, and kinked
Follicles all textured of every hue
My laughter cries
Alabaster asbestos tears
Prism pure carving out my patriotic valley
From sea to cancerous sea
This is my country, too

I Can't Find My Music

I can't find my music.
The music in me has become
A case of mistaken identity…
Is my McClurkin in my Jock Jams?
Is my Janice in my J. Lo?
Is my Michael in my Usher?
Is my Jesse in my M.L.K?
Is my B.B. King Snoop doggin' in my Romeo?
Is my Diana disrespecting my Aretha?
Is my Ray Charles blinded by my Stevie?
I wonder?

War Talk

Time out, time out, time out
I will not cry uncle
I'm declaring a time out
So we can regroup
The casualties are one sided
In our war on racism
War on poverty
War on domestic violence
Our wars on whatever other
Walt Disney king of the hill G.I. Joe war games
We have been playing
The war on terrorism
Must have a different strategy
Than our failed war on racism
The war on terrorism
Must be fought with different tactics
Than our failed war on poverty
The war on terrorism
Must be pimp slapped
Differently than our war on domestic violence
I'm declaring a time out to
REGROUP!

Bent Over But Not Buried

It's a new warfare to be waged
When the enemy deals
primarily in guerilla suicide missions
Our brother and sister countries
are starting to whine about our rhetoric
If the enemy can have missions
then we can have crusades
If it seemed like for a moment
I wanted to bury my head in the sand
it would have only
Been to give the enemy
a better vantage point
from which to kiss my-----

For God and Country

I've been renewed
My soul has been rejuvenated
The inseams of my heart
have been retailer made to fit
My new American million-dollar diva.
So don't fret my children
I will protect you
With the ferociousness of a
Lion hearted sphinx.
Come on super women
Join me
Bring your Tarzan yells,
Join me!

A Man Thang

Over 4,000 dead, injured, maimed
Unaccounted for
And you want to play football
Is it a man thang
I can barely cook
Look at a skillet
The food is bland
I've tried dominos, ceasars, and long johns
I insisted they make it my way
And it still had no taste
But then again for me
Maybe it's a motherland thang
A Shirley Chisolm, Barbara Jordan, Rosa Parks
Statue of Liberty thang
And you want to play football!

It's On

Tag my sistah
You're it
You've been flagged
By your New York crimson babies
Fatherless, motherless
Tag you're it
You've been flagged
Registered, enlisted, initiated
Drafted into service
Hazed by terrorists
Tag
You're it
You've been flagged
Take your sons off the
New white lightening
Take them to the Ritalin Detox clinic
Put the fire back in their steps,
Your breast back in their mouths
Suckle them with the
Red, white, & blue of their patriotism
Tag, you're it,
Betsy Ross, meet Queen Latifah
The new mother of our nation

Sleeping with The Enemy

It is important that we
As the victims speak out
Say what ever we need
Do what we need to heal
But I warn you
Choose your needs wisely
Do not make choices
That are self-destructive
Choices that re-victimize
Choices that will cause us
to sleep with the enemy

Perforation of Love

No more news
No more tragedy
My round of reproduction
My feminine creative space
Can't take it
God the creator of all
Is this how you feel?
Empty, with perforated love?

Claustrophobia

I gotta get out
I gotta getout
I gottagetoutIgottagetoutIgottagetout

Middle Class America

As usual
the lines in Wal-mart
Were long
Big city traffic long
But no one cared
No one complained
It was just good
To be out, away
From the umbilical
Cord of the tragedy
We all looked at one another
constantly
as if we were
The walking dead
We searched one another's
Eyes looking for something
Something recognizable, all
American arrogance was gone
The arrogance that was
our patriotic right
Smoldered into vapor
At ground zero
A Wal-mart full

of unfocussed patriots
Looking for normalcy
Americans needing
to re-establish America
Looking for a dependable
patriotic character trait
Trying to be normal
Our leaders are saying go back to
Business as usual
So this Saturday,
5 days after
We will be normal,
We are Middle America,
The real America,
We will go to Wal-mart
We will spend our hard earned
patriotic cash
We will buy American
5 days after
We are taking a stand
We have bought
everything red, white, and blue
In all of the Wal-mart stores in America
Middle class power rules
We will be
normal again.

Just Buying a Pretzel at The Mall

From the back of their heads
I thought they were two Mexicans
With their two young daughters
Standing in line
To buy a pretzel.
What could be the hold up?
The two fathers kept wiping their
Foreheads
They were sweating profusely
The pretzel line was mournfully silent,
staring American
Torpedoes at the two
Who from the back of their heads
Looked like Mexicans
They turned to leave,
pretzel and lemonade
Clutched tightly in one hand
Wiping sweat with the other
Their two daughters
staring wide-eyed
At their daddies
Turned profile
I noticed then

why they were sweating
I knew then
they weren't Mexicans
were they Pakistani
were they Lebanese,
Saudi Arabian?
Egyptian?
Afghanistans?
Iranians?
Definitely not of Spanish descent
Were they Muslims?
Terrorists…
No America
Take a deep breath
As they passed me by
The daughters chattered away
In perfect down home
Appalachian southern drawls
Whew, just 2 fathers
Who probably get their daughters
every other weekend
just like most American
every other weekend Daddies
Just trying to buy a pretzel
at the mall.

Praying for Grace

What looked like
a Saudi Arabian man,
Asked a Wal-mart clerk
In a thick accent
Where are the sleeping bags?
He spoke like Gandhi
I immediately thought
"sleeping bags"
Something terrorist would buy
Oh Jesus, on bended knee,
I beg you to forgive me
For my new found prejudice

Tomorrow

Day six
I will wake up
from my fifth
Sleepless night
and
I will have
a new
normal day

Day 6

SUNDAY, SEPTEMBER 16, 2001

Finally I slept through the night...

Milk Toast Patriotism

Leaders
of the local communities
Are running scared
Scared to indict
Scared to incite
Pooh-poohing
the current massive patriotism
Doubting
the longevity of the peoples
Rally around the flag
It is said that George Bush
couldn't sustain
America's enthusiasm.
My patriotism,
my patriotic attire
My flag waving
is not in honor of
A man we call president
Let me inform you,
local elected officials
Have you forgotten,
I am the real America
Not the congress

Not my state representative
Not some Ivy League college dean
or poli-sci expert
ME
little ol'
My country tis of 'me'
Me
So move over
my milk toast sissy patriots
You are blocking the sun
from my flag

Day 7

MONDAY, SEPTEMBER 17, 2001

Are You My Enemy

Will the real enemy
Please stand up
Please stand up
Please stand up
Will the real enemy
Please stand up
Please stand up
Please stand up
Na-na, na-na, naaanaaaa
You didn't get me
You missed me
You missed me
Now you gotta kiss me

Use To

When I couldn't
make sense of things
I used to cut my hair
Change its color

It is Now

If ever my sistah patriots
We needed female input
It is now
Mothers
we must raise
a new nation
It is now
Hillary,
pull Bill's pants up
Shove him out the door
And tell him
the nation is waiting
for somebody
To stand up and be 'de man'
Women,
It is now
Teachers
we need to re-dedicate
and re-educate
Get our children off Ritalin
It is now
We need their hyper activity
You cannot be sedated

and win a war
You cannot be sedated
and combat terrorism
Teachers
It is now
Mothers
we need to eradicate
Drug wheelers and dealers
911 them
that the enemy's monies
are financed
Off of the drugs
in our sons and brothers veins
Before we can bust the enemy
We must come clean ourselves,
mothers
It is now
Not tomorrow
Waiting on today's yesterdays
It is now
Sisters, nieces,
daughters and aunts
God mothers, Grandmothers,
mothers
It is now

Who is My Neighbor

Are we living next to
friend or foe?
A turban
does not an enemy make
The Muslim child
in our classroom
Olive skinned
Ebony hair
Is not the target
Check,
ch-check yourselves America
Don't let us repeat
The concentration camps
of yesterday
Learn our lessons
and make a better move
This is a new day dawning
And we mustn't
go into the night
Yawning

Drafting Women

The glass ceiling has been broken
The good ol' boys club
Is now open for membership
Womenist/feminist
What ever your shading
Quit fiddling with your bras
Let's get busy
Doing what
Women warriors
of past wars did
Doing what they did
during Desert Storm
WW II
The Korean War
WW I
The Civil War
The Revolution
If you can't do nothing but sew
Sew a flag
There's already a shortage in America
Let us fill it with the red, white, and blue
Passion granted us as one nation under God

The Civil Squirmish

Put out the fires
Of our inner skirmishes
The domestic civil warfare
Between the red, white and blue
If I have a hatchet
Consider it buried
Beneath the rubble of the towers
If there was a bone to pick
It is clean, burnished by the flames
of an enemy airplane
Black America
George needs help
Even if we didn't put him there
America is more ours than his
He is in the white house
As a squatter
A temporary tenant
We are America's realtors
Our mammies,
Our pappies
Our Carvers and Dubois'
And Douglass' and Brown's
Our eggs fertilized the sperm

of an ever
Greater George
A man deemed the father
of our country
But who is our mother?
Some vivacious choco-latte
Keeping house
in the slave quarters

Shout Mammy Shout

I am not a serious collector of anything, but I do own a few Black Mammy knick-knacks. They remind me that there could never have been a 'That's So Raven' without Moms Mabley. Today's Oprah, or a Barbara Jordan or a Maya Angelou could never have existed without yesterday's Butterfly McQueen, Aunt Jemima or Phyllis Wheatley. There is no Beyonce without Diane Carroll and Mahalia Jackson.

The incentive for my Mammies began with my family when I was in high school. Every weekend our family raced to see who could find the "best" garage sale. The two unspoken criteria for the "best" garage sale were that it (1) had to have things you could purchase or barter down to a dollar and (2) it had to have things that another member in the family would like.

My four brothers and I would take off in every direction on our bikes on Saturday morning going on the hunt. What we really tried to find were Black whatnots to add to our parents collection. We would carefully bicycle home with jet black Mammy sugar bowls, deep ebony Sambo salt shakers, wide-lip grinning watermelon eating toothpick containers and buck eyed out house using napkin holders proudly hidden in our lint filled pockets or tucked under our sweaty armpits. All pieces of America's historical past proudly purchased for a dollar or less.

Recently I saw a similar cast iron Mammy door stop I had purchased for what I thought was an overpriced two dollars at a white woman's garage sale in the 70's, for over two hundred dollars at a peddlers market junk shop. I have traveled, taught, performed and spoken in 37 of our marvelous United States.

Throughout my career I have been dumbfounded by America's value system. I am ashamed at the inequity of the intrinsic value of a joyous watermelon seed skeeting piece of Americana porcelain compared to the same devalued likeness sitting in time-out at the back of the classroom on "mind altering" attention deficit medication.

I am truly bamboozled at the jacked up price of a buck eyed, nappy headed sketch of a purple black naked girl sitting on a spittoon with a roll of toilet paper at her feet compared to the devalued naked grinning girls exposing themselves on Black Entertainment Television. The Black woman 'in mammy form' used to govern many white households, determining its moral values, insuring that it ran as a well-oiled and fine tuned patriotic family machine.

Now Black women are stereotypically portrayed as mysterious boodie shaking, baby making, over indulging sex machines. These imbalanced ideologies and vulgar portrayals of a God-breathed people bring Holy Temple destructing, inflamed anger to the very fiber of my African American soul. It makes my ancestral insides wanna SHOUT, SHOUT, SHOUT!!!

Shout Mammy Shout

A real black woman
Is obsessed possessed
We're hungry mean
Braggadocious egotistical
And why not for
Who else will
Applaud us
Stand by us
Pick us up?
We up pick ourselves
Stand on our knees in prayer
Clap at our own delight
And we
Shout,
Shout,
Shout,
Shhhhhh--ou--outs!!!!

It Sure Was Beautiful

You ever have lots
Of something
But it ain't all
Kept in one spot?
People say you're a
Collector and
You say you're not
You just got a lot
Of the same thing
Different colors
Different shapes
In different positions
But just not kept
In the same place
In the house
10 butterflies
7 salt and peppershakers
8 glass turtles
16 depression era lamps
But that doesn't make you a
Collector
Collectors
Organize

And arrange and
Display and talk
About their stuff
My stuff is just stuff
Stuff that tickles my fancy
But I have to be honest
One day I took all of my books
By Black folks out of a box
Stacked them on a shelf
Next to all of my porcelain mammies
And jig-a-boo men fishing,
Eating watermelons and
Peeking out of outhouses
I stepped back
Took a long look…
And it sure was beautiful.

Nobody Knows
The Nappy Headed Bluegrass Blues
I've Seen

I've got the alphabet blues
I've got the alphabet blues
I've got the alphabet blues
Oh baby, oo-ah-ooooooo
Ain't got nobody to talk to blues
All my children blues
Ain't yo' mama on the pancake box blues
Anxiety attack blues
Abscessed tooth blues
All night blues
Banana boat blues
Bikini blues
Blood sucking, black balled
Blue grass
Breastfeeding
Buh-buh-buh-baby blues
Cellulite blues
Countryside blues
Candlelight blues
Chestnuts roasting on an open fire blues

Count your many blessings name them one by one blues

Oh baby, oo-ah-ooooooo

Destiny child blues

Drama queen blues

Drivin' miss daisy with a man who is too

Dumb to ask directions blues

Everything ain't goin my way

Expect nothing and I'll never get disappointed

Egg salad

Evil eye blues

Oh baby, oo-ah-oooooooooooooooooo

I've got the fantail fanny Mae

Frightened out of my mind

Friendless friendships

Freaky Friday

Forever yours blues

Ground hog blues

Ginger Rogers was what made Fred Satire, Fred Astir blues

Ho-jo Howard Johnson blues

Halleluiah

How many times have I told you to put your

Hand over yo' mouth blues

Ice blue

Iris blue blues

Irritated blues

I done the best I knows how blues

Is you is or is you ain't my baby blues

Jupiter Jumpin' Jehosaphat

Jesus was a Jew

Ja-ja-jamin' blue blues

Oh baybee-oooo-ah-ooooooo

Kankakee jailhouse
Keynote speaker
Kangaroo punched
Kissin' cousin
Lady ga diva,
Liver,
Full voluptuous licking kissy-lip lovin'
May to December mid-life crisis blues
Military blues
Midnight train to Georgia blues
Messiah blues
Morning side blues
Mahbabydonegoneandlefmeforsompobackwaterwhitetrash
Oh baby, oo-ah-oooooo
Nobody loves me
Nobody remembered my birthday
Nobody knows the nappy-headed blues I've seen
Open minded, closed door
Over the river and through the woods to grandmother's house
I go
Omniscient, omnipresent, omnipotent
Only the lonely survive
Polka dotted
Power ranger
Praise the Lord
Peacock passionate blue blues
Quiet
Quite the contrary
Quickening quivering thighs
Oh baby, blue-blue-blues
Rustic rusty elbow

Round the mountain
Realizing
Rushed to the hospital blues
Sssssssssexy sistah
Six, six, six
Sick to my stomach
So sorry Mr. Charlie
Titillating, tantalizing
Trusting the untrustworthy
Blue-ah-oooooooze
Uncola nut
Unspiritual
Underwear hanging off yo-butt, showing yo booty
Used up love
Varicose vein
Worrywart
Wonder what tomorrow's gonna brang
Xerxes my brotha and xylophone the only words with
"X" I ever used
Year after year yo' mama
A to Z, African alligator, Zambia, zealous
Alphabet
Bluuuuuuuuuuuuu-ah-ooze

The Scarf

America wouldn't be America
if not for the diversity of the
head-scarf wearin' Black woman.
We are as soft as we are hard,
as intellectual as we choose to play coy,
as bending as we are straight.
Who can look good in jeans and a head rag
and then take that same scarf,
tie it around her waist and cook a meal
that will make any man slap his mamma
and his grandmamma too,
THEN toss that same scarf over one shoulder
step into church and shout, shout, shout!!!

Committee of One:
Tribute to Sonia Sanchez

On the eve of Dr. Martin Luther King, Jr.'s birthday
At the white college president's gorgeous plantation home
I supped of Ms. Sanchez' soul,
I embraced her hands,
I didn't want to let go,
It was as if there were answers there,
In her hands.
Hands that had touched a multitude of Rosa Parks
I touched furniture that she touched
I tried to tip toe my size tens
In her petite giant steps
That left dainty imprints
In the white college president's plush carpet,
I was allowed to breathe the same air she breathed,
Her small button nose that had smelled the blood of the King,
I was allowed to listen to the sounds she was listening to
Her ears having heard the dreams of a dreamer,
My soul felt unworthy next to hers.
What can I do to step up to the plate?
To qualify,
To give back?
I heard her thunder-whisper

Recalling her question and answer session
With the audience
In my spiritual ear,
"…just stand tall, stand erect, be human,
be human and black."
She spoke of making a change through
Forming committees.
Today, Martin Luther King's birthday,
I stood tall
Stood erect
Stood human
And black
And I became…
A committee of one

Watershed Woman

She slowly emerged with the
Glory sparkle of water and
Laughter on her hair
The caress of the Son upon her shoulders
Tendrils of
Waterweeds and river pearls graced
Her body bejeweled in the beauty of
Rainbow radiance
She stepped on shore
A hush came upon the river
One lonely bird serenaded
From its empty nest.
She donned a power suit
The water moaned and sighed
She walked in queenly dignity
Waited at the bus stop of life
Precious water dripping rainbow drops
From her briefcase
Men bumped into themselves
Women stared in envious disbelief
Eyes of children followed her
Guarding and protecting her.
In the elevators everyone

Gave space
Afraid to touch her aura.
Men in the boardroom
Clung to her every word
Peace was made
At her bidding.
She shed one tear on a memo and
Children were fed, clothed
And played with
Close, nearby and
At the far ends of the earth.
Because of the sweat from her brow
Flowers grew in the asphalt jungles.
With the licking of an envelope
Vegetation was released
From weeds of imprisonment.
The day grew long for Watershed woman
The river sent
A dog whistle alarm
For her return
The Son sent a migraine
For her return
The birds chirped frantically
For her return.
The elevator crowded her in
Smelling of the rottenness of foul souls
Men and women jostled her on the streets
Causing her to trip.
She needed water.
Clean clear 'unchemicaled'
Not the urine smell water of

Man's water fountains.
She must find water.
The pool at the park
Mocked her with drug deals and
Risqué rapings of unwilling
Little girls posed as women
The ride home found her bedraggled
Soiled and unkempt
Like a perpetual junky
She was thrown off the bus early
Folks laughed and pointed.
She started stumbling the wrong way home
It was the serenade of the mourning
That echoed her back on track
A crow cawed in remorse
Vultures circled
The water valley whispered love notes
That dropped tears for the return
Of their virgin daughter.
She shed her business world garb
Reviving at the familiarity of nakedness
And stumble-walked desperately
Back into her liquid nature.
The children of the day
Stood at the waters edge
Way into the dawn of the night
And into the ebb of the morning
Picking up cans and rusted metal
Sipping the dregs from broken teacups
Eating fast food trash
Taking shelter in the grave yard of

Discarded tires, retired dryers, car crumbs
And wounded truck beds
Waiting one more again
For her return

Poem-a-liscious

I loved a man
With golden tongued
Words that slurped
Down the corner
Of his chin
Sugar poems sparked
From his eyes
As he invented lies
That nudged at
My thighs
I slept
With his every rhyme
His promises
Temporarily drugged
My loneliness
Sedated my anxieties
Gave me temporary beauty
Gave me temporary esteem
Temporary justification
Until I realized
Every woman on the block
Every woman on the job
Every woman in the choir

And half the usher board
Was under the spell of my
Poem-a-licious pimp
Who hung out in the street corners of their heart
Cause he's so…so…
Poem-a-licious

Miss Ida Mae

This relationship
Stormed into my life
He changed the essence
of my lonely heart
When he stole a dozen roses
From old lady Ida Mae's
prize rose bushes
And gave them to me with his
Winning smile
He changed the essence
Of my car,
when I let him use it
Every day to drive me to work
He changed the essence
of payday
When I spent half my paycheck
On new clothes for him
To coordinate ever so nicely with me
He changed the essence
of my home
With his smell
Even though he's
Three days gone

His smell is still attached but
I know he's
Picking stolen roses from
Somebody else's prize bushes
He's driving some other woman's car
After he drops her off at work
And he's spending some other
Woman's paycheck
Five days gone
I drove myself home
Wearing a suit
That was his favorite color
I microwaved frozen lasagna
Left over from him...
Then I tossed it in the garbage
Piping hot
Called the car dealership
About a trade in,
Next morning
His favorite color suit
was staring at me
On the bedroom floor
I dropped it off at the goodwill box
As I drove home in my
New used car...
Five weeks gone
I was back to reading my Bible
At night before I went to bed
And a dried rose petal
Fell from the pages
I stuck it in an envelope

I wrote, "Please forgive me"
For the return address
I ordered three-dozen pink roses
And mailed them to
Old lady, Miss Ida Mae.
I no longer count the days gone
'Cause more importantly
"I'm" gone!

Left Behind #1

Voices of the heart
Whisper, "Wait,
Don't leave me so
Lovers she prepared to
Shine and show
She's left behind
While others go
Left behind
So others will know
The potential of love
The squalor of hate.
She's left behind
Not because she's late.
A 'light' walking woman
Who embraces fate
Left behind
Because going
Can't wait!

Left Behind #2

Sweat poured
Nobody ignored
What happened that day
It still
Won't go away
Dragging a cross
The world at a loss
There's no way He'd die,
Forgiveness good by
Last turn and wave
A surrendered soul
With keys to the grave.

One Fork

After 10 years of marriage
I woke to one fork
A drawer full of spoons
Three pairs of panties
A drawer full of brassieres
But only one fork
Plenty of bras
left from breast-feeding
Plenty of spoons
from the children's food transition
But only one fork
I ponder the imbalance
Of a meatless relationship
Nothing that would require fork talk
No lacy adornments
For my nether hither lands
He doesn't even journey there any more
At last visit
My pumpkin patch was gently black
Now it rides as sprigs of wisdom white
Even if he did stop by again
Between the shifts and sags
Dimples and bags he'd swear

He was making sex to another woman
I resolve to
Buy more panties
And they won't say
Monday
Tuesday
Wednesday
Thursday
Friday or
Saturday
No
I'll open several underwear bags
And just buy the Sunday panties
I'll trim them in lace
And I'll hot glue
Some diamonds on those bad girls
Then I'll go to the Dollah sto'
And get me
Some mo'
Forks.
Cause we all know,
a real fine dressed lady,
owns more than just one fork.

Pretty Hands

I forgot I have
Pretty hands
Men use to always
Comment on my hands
They said they
Were magically beautiful
Healing
Comforting
When I touched other things
One boy even said he wished
He were the other things
He actually said
Things I touch
Make him jealous
Now that's real romantic
Unless he was lying
But I don't think so
Children are proof of the touch
When children wait in line
Or at your desk
Or sneak up around you
For you to touch them
Then you definitely do have
Pretty hands

Oops

Oh thunder!!!
A thought dripped
Out of my brain
And spilled
Out of the corner of
My mouth
Before my heart could
Catch it and polish it up
Or send it back

Now I have to
Apologize
But I won't mean it

Same Sex Lament #1

To my close gay brothas
Femininity is the God given melody
of my womansong
God-given glint of my girlishness
The God-notes of my tears
The celestial lace of my laughter
Ocean front reflection
of my property pearls
Femininity is the starfish joy
of my preoccupation with diamonds
Divine femininity
is my unique monthly identity
With the shedding of the blood
of God's Son.
It is not and cannot be
a cross gender thing
Its ways are often
aped and masqueraded
But God-given femininity
is divinely appointed.

Same Sex Lament #2

Things and things
and such and such
Subject matter shhhhhhh,
don't touch
A sex change
no more a woman makes
Than a black millionaire
A white person makes
Than a painted moth
A butterfly makes
Than a tuxedo
on an ostrich
A penguin makes
Things and things
and such and such
Subject matters shhhhhhhh,
don't touch

Denial

This wasn't a fly by night
A one-night hump
A booty call that went bad
This was over 11 years of
Inner investments
Soulistic expenditures
Making denial
A healthy out.
Because reality would mean
Division
Lied on lies
Refracted souls
Yours versus mine
You did and I didn't
And you didn't and I did
Broken investments
Unmendable memories
Words of permanence
Death.
Denial
It's a good thing
It will turn 11 years
Into 12, 12 years into 25,

Surprise!!!
My 50th wedding anniversary
Denial is my friend she has been
Very, very, good to me.

Church Kill

Christians driving
their lean mean
If you dare
soul winning machines
Joy riding
down the road of life
Really frilly faith
Aw shucks, do I have to faith
I-I-I-…look at me-me-me faith
Virgin faith
Blinded
in their holier than thou headlights
Crushed
under their earthbound chariot wheels
Blocking the pews
of renewal
Sedated
by the same ol' same ol'
Driving in cruise control
On the highway
to hell

Not In My Dictionary

What is petty?
There's no room
for petty
When you work
two full time jobs
There's no such thing
as petty cash
To a forever
broke family
Petty?
Wasted space
in an ebonics dictionary

I Goes to Church
(A Tribute to My Grandmother)

On Monday
I goes to Monday church
On Tuesday
I goes to Tuesday church
On Wednesday
I goes to Wednesday church
On Thursday
I goes to Thursday church
On Friday
I goes to Friday church
On Saturday
I get my hair
and nails done did
My clothes washed
My car aromatized and samsonized
So that on Sunday
After skimming my Sunday school lesson,
Tying 2 quarters in the corner of my hanky
For mission offering, stuffin'
5 dollars in my bosom for tithes,
And one dollar in my bible to slip the preachur…
I goes to church

God Knew

I look around
And
God knew what
He was doing
And even if God was a She
Cause there
Are
She
Images all over the place
(As a matter of fact
More she's than he's.
God still knew
What She
Was doing.
You don't have to
Argue the point
Cause, there are more fleas
Than he's
Could it be/
God is a …
I just accept that…
God knew.

Nothing Lonelier

There's nothing lonelier than
A full moon on a dark winter's night
Unless
It's the naked limbs of a tree surrounded by pollution and
blight
Or a sterile pond, that lost the fight
Or the howling wind whipping an empty swing
Back and forth with empty delight
Or a deaf owl that
Yearns to make contact
Or child waiting for daddy to appear
While mother stands guard real near
Or the tail of a rat
Left uneaten by a cat
One just can't get any
Lonelier than that

Millennium Feminism

Come!
Here we go again
One frazzled woman at a time
Dragging her tired ta-tas in
An untucked blouse tag
A breakfast stain
left over from dinner
Empty eyes
searching for a meaning
The looks with out looking,
the stares without seeing the movement
The mowed movement of feminism
masquerading as women
Polite women in angry bodies
Tired bodies,
Wanna be humans
With the claws of humane-ness
clutching the setting sun of their breasts
The chicky girls and
The Barbie dolls
The mannish girls and
The hard core whores of feminism
Embracing to become clean

To become one
All with a ticket
to the Titanic ride of life
Anchors away
Black pride
White pride
Gay pride
Gray pride
The deflowering of feminism
Was it only a fad?
But it is crucially important
that my daughters
Be there

The World Went Crazy

When blakk women stopped shouting
At first little things changed
Hearing became deaf to
The sweet aroma of prayer
The widow's mite became
A bug that made blakk women scratch in their hair
Cornbread became something made in a jiffy from a box
Country homes had to invest in locks
When blakk women stopped shouting
Children carried faces of pouting
There was no place to go for a hug
and a good wisdom fussing
Time sped up, sending generations rushing
No more a dose of wisdom or upon a time, once
Folks couldn't tell a biscuit from a sconce
When blakk women stopped shouting
Elvis permanently left the building
Cotton shacked with polyester
Perm-a-press came on the scene
Fashion evolutes and bodies
Became polluted with leisure suits
Geri-curls, earth shoes, hip huggers
Tattoo paints

Permanent indigestions, acid reflux
Carpel tunnel all sorts of wimp diseases
Sniffles and sneezes
Cause recipes, potions, roots and notions got lost
When blakk women stopped shouting
Blakk women stopped shouting
Preachers started outing
The world was full of abominations
And big story sensations
Blakk women stopped shouting
The super bowl became rated X
Folks started worshipping tyrannosaurus rex
Oh blakk women
Go back to your past
We need a good hallelujah
And a 'help me holy ghost'
An ummm…mmmmmmmmm and a 'mercy'
Cause the world is terribly lost
Shouting women come back
We need you at all cost
Blakk women could jump the pews
Change the headlines of the Monday daily news
Making a rascally man go right
Before he shot some body on Monday night
What can we do blakk women
To bring you back to your command
To hear you sang
Precious lawd take my hand
To make the president understand
Just one more time
Put your hands on your hips

and let your back bone slip
Throw your head back far then spread
Your arms to heaven then zoom to the alter
Like a shooting star
Shiny wigs start to flying but purses stay close and tight
And the feet start Holy Ghost dancing
To the left and to the right
Hands grab your back and then circle round
Shouting to heaven then down to the ground
Then silence, the sound of one passed out
The spirit tags another as shout echoes and mounts
All the way to heaven as scripture unfurls
To provide another week of safety in the world
But since blakk women stopped shouting
And left white folks' houses
Children get drugged at school
And terrorists, adulterers and fools lead nations
The world flat went crazy
Values went hazy, morals got lazy
When blakk women stopped shouting

THUNDER...

I Ain't Scared

Old folks taught young folks
To be scared of thunder
But I'm not
I talk on the phone
In the middle of a storm
But I won't run across the cotton field
Or go get the cows from the back forty
I got some sense
Not much
But I got some sense
I have one of those
Special plugs for my computer
But I'm not scared of thunder
I just prefer not to lose my stuff
I've jumped
My heart has pounded like a jackhammer
Once I even ducked a little
I fear thunder
Carry a healthy respect
Like I respect God,
I have a fear of disappointing Him
But I ain't scared like the old folks
I ain't scared.

Bring On The Thunder

Love me as me
With leaps and bounds
Celebrate
My noiseless joy.
Bring on the thunder.
God gave me lightening for earrings.
Brrrrr-ing on the thunder.
The purrr-fecting sound of love

The Whole Truth
And Nothing But The Truth

Hear the slow whisper
roll of thunder
How painful truth is
Smell the coffee stains of rain.
We'd much rather
Cohabitate with
Little white lies
And splash around in
The Jacuzzi of self-denial
Rather than living in
The whole truth
and nothing but the truth
So help us God.
The rain pounds
and massages the earth
Thunder has arrived

There Used to Be Mo Rainbows

I met a man who had only seen a rainbow
In a coloring book
Where have all the rainbows gone
Siphoned into bottles of nail polish one be one
Mahogany metallic
Heather hi-shines
Elusive emeralds
Radical rubies
Sacred sapphires
Amorous amethysts
To be displayed on a small make-up table
Reflected in a pool of 60 watt illumination
That's where all the rainbows have gone
In hiding with miniature paint brushes
To anoint the tips of little girls fingers
Pretending to be
Mother nature rainbow queens
With their pink Barbie doll plastic wands
That's where all the rainbows have gone

Same Spirits

The same spirit
whispers around
The Eiffel tower
And The Golden Gate Bridge
Around
The sheet music of Handel's Messiah
And
The paint chips of
Michael Angelo's church mural
Around
Picasso's empty spaces
As inside the spray cans
full of gang graffiti
It's the same spirit an apple
The entire sum of its parts
The same spirit that cries
Where have all the buffalo gone

Ends of The Earth

I've been to
the ends of the earth
Misguided loyalties
Fake royalty
A baby's last breath
We told you so
Down right dirty dog
Best friend got my man
All that is good in me
Traded for reality TV
And notarized lies.
I've been to
the ends of the earth

Notarized Liars

Heads of states
Governments and such
Preachers
Folks with clout
Who knows
what they be talkin' about
They call a wrench--pliers
And we vote after all
For the best
notarized liars

Dream Catchers

Unmade beds
Are like unmade dreams
All for naught
For how soon
they evaporate
And how regularly quick
Night comes
And we climb
once again
Into
unmade beds

The Thunder Sermon

It is said throughout history:
The best strategies for conquering a nation
is to destroy, undermine, negate,
denigrate, humiliate,
and demolish its women.
Are you feeling destroyed my sisters?
Are you feeling undermined my sisters?
Are you feeling negated
and denigrated and humiliated?
Are you feeling unpolished and demolished?
It seems that unless we women
get back up off of the floor,
and start walking out the door
and crawl out from under the bed
and come out of hiding from behind the shed,
It is my horrible fear
America as God knows it
will surely disappear.
What ever happened to
"I am woman hear me roar
In numbers too big to ignore"
Meow, meow, meow
Roar women roar

Roar women roar

rrrrrrrrrroooooooooaaaaaaaarrrrrrr

Were we too busy

shooting the messenger

That the message

blew away in the rain

Stop being a kitty cat and roar

like the ovarian lioness that you are

Not just for your children's sake

but for

Your own sake

Besides who ever said that Thunder

was not a woman

Clapping her thighs shut

Shaking her hair dry

Giving birth to

the Son of Man

RRRRRRROOOOOOOOAAAAAAARRRRRRR

RRRRRRROOOOOOOOAAAAAAARRRRRRR

RRRRRRROOOOOOOOAAAAAAARRRRRRR

Kissin Cousin

Thunder finds
Comfort with
The kissing cousin kinship of
The black woman
Thunder plays hide and seek
In the blood of a black woman
In the hug of a black woman
In the eyes of a black woman
In the thighs of a black woman
Snub her
Take her for granted
Ignore her
Her gossamer web will cocoon you
Her thunder will
Entwine you with
Electrical shocks
And…
You'll never know
What happened
You'll never be the same
Her thunder draws
Come close
Touch her

Caress her
Bow to her
And…
She'll lift you up
With the thunder
Of her power.
Her thunder repels
But you always come back
For one more encore
For one more
Thunderous
Applause.

Chunks of Me

I'm disturbed
I'll break.
No one will notice
All the crumbs of me
Scattered
The chunks of me
Spattered across the sidewalk.
They'll step over me
As if I'm not there
Just like when I was
Still stuck to me
Folks bumped, side-stepped,
Lived around me
As if I wasn't there

Thunder and Me

We've decided
That it's okay.
My thunder side
Gains power in my obscurity
No one can measure
the power of thunder
Until she
Decides to reveal herself
The might is in the potential for
The decision:
The moment before
Thunder purrs
And
The moment after
Folks pick themselves up
off of the ground.
So, we've decided that
It's okay
Just keep on
Not noticing us,
Thunder and me

Secret Hiding Places

I knew a girl
who swallowed batteries
To see if they would turn her
into the Energizer bunny
I knew a girl
who hid crayons in her vagina
Cause she didn't have any at home
Poverty makes quite an artistic statement
It is an exact science
I loved winter
When all of our clothes from the closet
Were laid on top of us to keep us warm
The smell
Of uncle daddy's work shirt musk
Of garage oil, camphor phenique
and starlight peppermints
And momma's bacon greased apron
On top of the aroma
of her lilac toilet water
Sunday dress
An old mangy suffocating
black wool sweater that
I picked white lint balls off of

Like counting sheep
until I fell asleep
That girl didn't turn into the
Energizer bunny
She just passed the batteries
Secretly out her butt
But the girl who hid
Crayolas in her vagina
Draws beautiful pictures
and hides them secretly
Under my bed.
Everybody knows
the best place to hide things
Is under your bed,
in your mouth,
or in your vagina

But I Don't Believe In Reincarnation

Do you ever feel
Cremated
And that
You've been sprinkled
Onto
The baptism of
A
Newly undead?

Death Around Me

I heard death around me.
A low-pitched
Screeching sound
A silence visited by a
Sudden thud
Then a loud soft thump.
I heard a chunk of my brain
Floating down the sidewalk
Then get stuck at the drainage ditch
Allowing me the grace to think
One more thought
And the only thought
I could muster was,
"Wow, I can't believe
I had the courage to jump"

Night Don't Count

A shadow is the last poverty of hope
The last perhaps the last what if
The last if what
The last maybe just
The last just maybe
But on days
When there is no shadow
Hope is gone.
But night don't count
Cause
I have seen
My shadow
In the inner city
On a winter's starry
Christmas Eve night

Black Assurance

Shadows are always black
And everybody's got one
Ever seen a white shadow?
If you did
Twas a
Ghost!

I Remember When

I remember when
All girls were sisters
And we touched each other
And we walked holding hands
And we carried messages to a boy
For a girlfriend
And we could
And would
Keep a secret
And we only stretched the truth or lied
For the better good
Of the sisterhood
I know this wasn't a dream
Cause
I remember when
All girls were sisters
And we touched each other
And we walked holding hands

This Side of Abraham's Covenant

Monet
Moneta Sleet, Jr.,
the Pulitzer Prize photographer
Bach
B.B. king and his Lucille symphonies
Dolly Parton's original boobs
Janet Jackson and Jennifer Lopez'
original buttocks
Lucille Ball
Moms Mabley
Sir Lawrence Olivier
Sir Sidney Poitier
William Shakespeare
Spike Lee
Ed McMahon
Arsenio Hall
Telly Sevales and "Who loves ya, baby?"
Duke Ellington and "Love you madly"
What is this world coming to?
It's coming to…
Abraham's tomorrow…today

Some Thoughts

Some thoughts should
Always, always, always,
Remain…
Where the thunder hides

The Toast

A drunken white man told me once
The first words he learned to read
Was a sign that said
"for white's only"
He started to cry
One of those deep sobbin', sloppy
Ugly faced high pitched girlie cries
Took another long sip
Baptizing the ugly exposure
of his vulnerability
He slobbered,
"The only mother I really ever-ever had
Was a blue-black bronze mammy woman
My own mother was too fragile, too busy,
Too dignified, too...too
To let me drink from
her homogenized lily breasts.
But not Muhdeah, what I wouldn't give
Today to suckle at her full richness,
Muhdeah's deep pillowed
Lush, soothing, land of Eden bosom,
Not in a sexy way, but in a mother to son
Son to mother, Muhdeah sort of way.

She tasted of evaporated sweet milk
Of thick coffee cream,
of fresh churned thick brown butter Hershey kisses"
He sobbed,
"The only girl I ever loved, was her daughter
My 'Netta…Netta was, well, she was my 'Netta
She listened deep, through her eyes
And she could make me laugh at anything
And cry at the beauty of every thing.
To…My 'Netta,"
He toasts,
"and…and…and all of the beautiful
Colored girls of the world. She didn't want to,
So I took her…and plunged myself into her deepness.
She stopped listening to me through her eyes
That night. She never invited me to laugh
With her again, She was the last
Beautiful thing I saw worth crying about."
He stood up, drank, as if to the honor of a queen,
Rumbled through his wallet
Cursed then said,
"Here 'tis."
He kissed it.
"I kiss it every night
Her picture, here, here,
isn't she wonderful, see her deepness?
Can you see it?
Here, take it, take it, I want you to have it.
'Cause you're so deeply beautiful."
He stumbled from the room.
Vomited in the hall and staggered away.

I looked at the picture a long, long time.
Crinkled, cracked,
yellow-taped in two places, a corner missing,
I could see the deepness in her eyes
Even I would have loved her
Photo, frozen in innocence…
so many years ago…
So many, many, many years ago…
Of…me.

I Really Like Me

When I calm down
And…
When I settle into my self
I really like me.

I Thundered

I saw a 5-year-old white boy
Put a cigarette in his mouth
I thundered
I saw 2 black boys grab
A white woman's purse and run
I thundered
I saw a Latino boy
violating a little black girl
I thundered
Everyone else looked away
But I stood on the sidewalk
And I thundered
And I thundered
And I thundered
The little white boy froze,
The cigarette
dropped from his mouth
A black woman
helped the white woman up
And with her 2 sons in hand,
returned the white woman's purse
The little black girl bit the Latino
Boy in his privates,

She thundered,
Brushed herself off
Winked over her shoulder
At my memory
And I walked away
In the lightening
Of the healing quiet
After the storm

Psalm 81:7

Thunder hides
at the bottom of my drink
Where the straw meets
It dances at the tip of my pen
And between my eraser crumbs
Thunder plays
beneath the delete button
On my Macintosh
She bathes in the aromatic
Urine smells
Of the nursing home
Thunder hangs
out at the secret back door
Of abortion clinics
Her name is still on the attendance books
At Columbine High school
Never to graduate
She skateboards on the oil slicks of
Her polluted oceans
We are the
Cinema that thunder watches
Raining in the tears of our miseries
Clapping to the joys of our victories

Laying her down to sleep
In the stuck together pages
Of the unused family bible
Cry to her when you are in trouble
And she will save you
She lives on Mount Sinai
That's where she hides
Oh thunder
Oooooh thunnnnnnndeeeer
Come out, come out
Where ever you are.

*W*hat happened? What changed Black America? Was it watching Rodney King take every Black man's beating...over and over and over again in instant replay...week after week? Was that suppose to scare us...teach us a lesson? In my presence my white liberal friends acted appalled. But several of those same liberal friends were whispering on the inside, "Hit him again, harder...harder...yeah, I can tell by the sound of that one-- that was a good hit."

The Rodney King episode instilled a new sense of white power. I wonder where those cops are now. I also wonder, where were Rodney's Mama, and sisters and aunties and girl friends? Where were the Black women in Rodney's life the night he was out getting his behind kicked by the white boys?

THUNDER...
Can you hear me?

Words

Words don't work in a vacuum
Sucked in between
two cardboard covers
Words are to be kissed out
They explode
on the scene of joy
Vomit in a firework of anger
The unspoken word is just that
Unspoken non-speak
Illiterate unreading
Breeding depressed paranoia
Ungraced esteem
less alienated distorted life
Blinded by silence
Untouched by the complimentary
I LOVE YOU
YOU'RE THE GREATEST
I MISS YOU
COME TO SEE ME AGAIN
CAN I DO ANYTHING FOR YOU
Words aren't just words
They are power
The Word was with God

From the beginning of time
WHO LOVES YOU BABY
LOVE YOU MADLY
I LOVE YOU THIS MUCH
To speak or not to speak
Whether tis nobler to shut up
Or to share
It is the best of times
And the worst of times
Thunder…
Can you hear me?

Every Breath I take

There are days
I write poetry
Just…
To cope with breathing.

Anticipation

All of my pores are open
Exposed
Hypersensitive
Listening
To the beginning whispers of thunder
Anticipating its mighty growl
Portrayed in God's Ecstasy at woman's good
Portrayed as God's anger
in woman's disappointment
God's thunder
Nevertheless
Smirks at sonic boom imitations
God doesn't fly airplanes
His sound could never be contained in a jet
Skywriting is but a cobweb in the sky
Let me write with you God
With the broad strokes of your rainbow pen
My footnotes are in the stirrup of life
I have assumed the position of birthing
With much anticipation
Obedience written is my prayer
Praise documented is my sacrifice
Thunder, can you hear me?

Trade Monkeys

The ocean thunder
of my heart beat
Stomps in my ears like
Waves crushing
Longing for the moon.
Answers elude me
Daily tasks sustain me
As time ticks by
Competing against my ever
Yearning pulse.
Ah yes, now we have arrived
At the think and thin of it
Stink and win of it
No gray areas here
Only trade monkeys.

Against The Law

Thunder…I know you can hear me
For you are the only one listening
It should be against the law
For one woman
to tell another woman
She's being too sensitive
For one woman
to downplay another woman
with rhetorical questions such as
Are you sure you didn't imagine it
You're not gonna wear that are you
Why whatever do you mean?
These are the subtleties
of abuse that women pass
Down generation to generation
Keeping us girls from age to age
But I go to bed a woman
and I wake up a woman
Gone are my days of girlness.
So when you ask,
"How are we girls doing today?"
I'm not being rude
You are not talking to me
I won't be answering

Foolin Myself

When I play second fiddle
Convinced that's how
One makes good harmony
When an entertainer
Or TV channel
Dictates my hair,
My clothes,
My walk
I'm just foolin' myself--
Pretendin' I'm living
And livin' large.
Missing my mansion
Hanging out in the garage…foolin myself--
Being all that somebody else can be
Instead of living large as
Genuine me
I really need to know
How to stop foolin- myself
and living life off the bookshelf
With somebody else's chapters
And happily ever afters
I'm dying a fool
Foolin' myself.

Is Anybody Home

Dying,
crying bones
Festering,
weeping wounds
Reoccurring,
pity filled pains from the past
Braving
unbeatable battles
Burying
16 year old baby boys
Wasting,
worrying woes
Fighting
unforgiving foes
Is anybody home?
Jesus,
can you hear me?

Minor Things

Calming the ocean
Sending and silencing the seasons
Setting boundaries between day and night
Between winter and spring
Determining the edge of summer that falls
Into autumn
Stretching heaven over empty space
Hanging the earth in mid air suspended by nothing
Wetting and making the law for rain
Wrapping its heaviness
In the vapor of my clouds
And my clouds not splitting
Under the weight of its magnificent moisture
Spit shining the stars,
Buffing the moon
Shaking out the sun on a foggy day
Unfastening and blowing out the wind
Deciding lightening paths
Designing flakes of snow
These are the minor things I do
Just a whisper of my power
Who then can understand
My thunder?

It Takes Two

It is easy to be silent
And subordinate when
Man makes the right noises
And behaves as the ordinate one
Yet the scenario is flawed
from way back in Eden's glory.
The curse being:
A flawed Eve
can only raise a flawed man
For thousands of years
Generations upon generations
of flawed people existed
Then God inseminated a perfect man
Into a woman He found pleasing
Ending the curse,
renewing the covenant
Yet it takes two to make a promise
It takes two to keep a promise
Jehovah,
you have done your half
But it takes two
Thunder, don't cry,
I hear you

Stand

Stand up and walk
Don't cry…walk it off
Take it like a man but
Change it like a woman
Under your power suit
Wear power lingerie
The lingerie of your calling
Be it Victoria secret
or 100% cotton
And once a month
(at least)
Be proud to walk as
A full-bloodied female
And if we must cry…
Cry tears of peace
Women of thunder
Can you hear me?

Bring Your Slippers

A child is a broad
Sweep of nature's paintbrush
A child is a walking rainbow
A child is life's extreme
A child splashes
A child tiptoes
A child doesn't walk
She runs
And jumps
And falls down
And bounces back up
A child isn't minutia
A child is detailed
But not about details
Every now and then I slip
Into my child
I wear a pink appropriate
Lady's house slipper on the right
With a big brown fuzzy bear
slipper on the left
It confuses the cat
But my 19-year-old daughter says
"Mom, I like your slippers."

We must come as children
But we must march as women.
Let us be as colorful
as the rainbow is long
Ready for life's extremes
Let us be prepared to splash
Or walk lightly
Or run, fall, and get back up
Let us be detailed
without drowning in the minutia
Come... bring your slippers
For we will take turns
standing guard

Sounds of Thunder

(1)
The rape of a child
Flesh upon flesh
Sick flesh
Against
New flesh
Passing the
Sickness on
For another generation
(2)
I woke to the sound
of falling snow
And the gentle pitter-patter
of butterfly feet
On the runway of life
My ancestors whispered
Change…
change is a comin'
Change…
change is a comin'
And the train
ran underground
Picking up future souls of freedom

Bringing a newness
to a stained earth
Brought on
with the expectation of
Spring in the heat
of a new fallen snow
Change…
change is a comin'
Change…
change is a comin'
Ch-ange…change
Change, change
(3)
There's laughter
And then there's laughter
Lets make fun of
Ha-ha-ha,
I got you laughter
Tickle me mommy
tickle me laughter
Ouch
that's my funny bone laughter
Sniggle-giggle
little girl's laughter
Then there's laughter
Laughing full blooded
Full-blown
Blest be the tie that binds laughter
Bent over clutching your gut
Lean back hands akimbo
Chin up to heaven

Wouldn't take nothing for my journey
Congregational laughter
Laughter in church
Shhhhh…!!!
(4)
No don't squelch the God
Laugh, laugh, laugh
How do we manage to praise
Without laughter
How do we manage to love
Without laughter
We don't, we can't, and
I won't.
Laughter loves
Laughter renews, restores, reclaims
I won't let my laughter
Ridicule, destroy and hate
I will hug you with my laughter
Embrace you with the healing of it
Welcoming you into my arms
And we will laugh together
Like a clapping of our souls
Do you hear it?
Souls clapping?
Now that's laughter
A welcome sound to
The ears of God
And in our laughter
Thunder will finally hear us.
(5)
Change…

change is a comin'
Change
I will reach in my briefcase
I will put on my apron
And my head rag
Pick up my skillet
And my rolling pin
I will embrace my past
To enrich my present
In order to empower our
Future
And I will walk hand in hand
Shouting with thunder
Change…
change is a comin'
Change…
change is a comin'
Change…

Columbine Lunch Lady

BANG...BANG
TAT-A-TAT-TAT
BOOM, BOOM
"whadaya say now Cheerleader
take that and that
kick-kick, feel my steel toe boot
football boy you're not good enough to shoot
for you, a slow death
while you look me in the eye
and watch slowly as my spit drips
now die football hero, die
where's your team now?
Littered across the field
now to the principal
I'll need extra ammo, the big fat sow."
"Bobby?"
"Did some one call my name
stealing my 15 minutes of fame?
Get outta the way lunch lady
it's Thursday, go cook something
some goulash or hash
don't make me hurt you
you're my only good past

you never let me sneak by
with a cookie or bag of chips
you'd send me back for
macaroni, mystery meat and peas."
"Bobby?"
"Not now lunch lady, go away please, please
duck, lunch lady, go back to your lunch stool
you shoulda been the teacher
teaching them the golden rule.
"What are you doing, Bobby?
Game that gun, Bobbie.
Boy don't look at me like that
Don't you see me with this bat
Get your butt in the cafeteria
It's time for me to fix lunch
When I heard all that racket & the sirens
I said sure as shootin' that's Bobby,
I had a hunch
Put your daddy's gun down.
Let me fix you something to eat
I think I still got some of your favorite mystery meat
You're a good boy Bobby
Put the gun in my hand
That's okay, I won't take it
Bobby you know, now you're a man."
Bobby spoke in a whisper
"Kill me, kill me, I'm already dead
Kill me with your bat, one hard swing to my head."
"Hush up little boy
Let lunch lady give you a hug
today's not a good day to die"

Bobby's shoulders went up with a shrug
He followed her cut out sneakers into the cafeteria
She fed him as they chatted and ate out of the pot
surrounded by America's finest, megaphones and
a sharp shooter looking for his shot
when lunch lady stood up
50 rifles simultaneously took aim
she said, "Get out, I'm the lunch lady,
this is my 15 minutes of fame!"

Dance Mountain Dance:
The Faith of a Watermelon Seed

I've lived mustard seed faith
I've said move Mountain
And it moved
I've said mooooove Mountain,
And it moved
The mountain of gossip, deceit, cheating, and lies
The mountain of impatience and impertinence
The mountain of being the right color at the wrong time
The mountain of enemies
The mountain of spousal abuse and negligence
The mountain of birth, death, abortion
The mountain of my sins moved
But after the Mountain ranges moved
There was nothing
But empty
And a valley of aloneness and solitude
In my Mountain free world I discovered
God only meant the mustard seed to be
The starting point, not the end all, and be all
Of faith
Not the final parameters
But only the jumping off place

I took on the challenge
and with the faith of a watermelon seed
I whispered
"Dance, mountain, dance!"
The Mountain lifted her skirt and
Began to Waltz.
"Dance, mountain, dance!"
And the mountain began to Cha-Cha
It did the Merengue and the Macarena
"Dance, Mountain, Dance"
It twisted, it shouted,
It did the Pony Marony and the Skate
and the Monkey and the Frugue
It Pop-locked into the Robot and C-walked.
Just imagine
Me
With the faith of an avocado seed shouting
"Sing, mountain, sing"
And finding my slumber in a mountain lullaby
Or even the faith of a mango seed, and my saying,
Make love to me Mountain, make love…
Oh just the faith of it!

THE END
OF ONE ENDING...

"Thunder,
Come out, come out
where ever you aaaaaaaare!"

...STARTING
A NEW BEGINNING

SHOUT, YOLANTHA, SHOUT!!!

www.ingramcontent.com/pod-product-compliance
Lightning Source LLC
LaVergne TN
LVHW011324080426
835513LV00006B/190